THE NATURAL WORLD SOMERSAULTS

THE NATURAL WORLD SOMERSAULTS

ISBN 9781763653023

Walleah Press
South Launceston
Tasmania, Australia 7249

www.walleahpress.com.au
ralph.wessman@walleahpress.com.au

THE NATURAL WORLD SOMERSAULTS

Shaine Melrose

CONTENTS

ABOUT THE AUTHOR

I acknowledge the Kaurna people, Traditional Custodians of the land on which I live and write. Sovereignty was never ceded.

Shaine Melrose is a queer writer and retired gardener, living in the Adelaide hills.

Along with being longlisted for the Vice-Chancellor's Poetry Prize 2023 and shortlisted for the Judith Wright Poetry Prize 2022, their poems have been widely published.

Shaine also has a short collection, released by Friendly Street Poets in New Poets #23.

For Helen

Collective Memory

Coiled in my cells is history,
black loch, divided clan, coarse heather,
farmed croft, a wooden boat.
I am an Australian airman's German burial,
jack boots, red segments of flag, an emptiness
returned to Bealiba station.
I am imperial greed's claimed land
turned to dust, stolen from the First People.
In my blood, a shredded testament, rocks and sheep –
fleece of prosperity, dwindling bush, wild
Wimmera, coastal salt spray of Port Melbourne.
Oily rainbows, red bricks, sheet metal, passing
ships, a sapphire and diamond ring binds
midwife and New Hebrides missionary.
I am Seymour, droplets of Goulburn River.
I am the dead, the dying.

I am Blois, a village in France, Gippsland, Moe.
Sawn wood, hammer and plane handmade.
Ash of razed houses and plentiful bush,
life preserved by field of corn.
Generations in tents, before I was born.
I am terrestrial orchid, narrow creek passing
dairy and cow, faces pulled at the train,
memories my mother can no longer retrieve.
I am the damage from great grandfather walking
into the dam, flowing from grandmother,
to mother, to me.
I am a history of jagged fragments.
From silence I speak.

Summer 1970

Summertime creeps and bites. We don't fight it.
Flopped onto freshly cut grass we scream with laughter.
Dad's last day of teaching has finally passed.

Dawn breaks, we pile into the Holden HR,
three sleepy children, coastal daydreams.
Up front, News Radio talks of war, our baby cries.

Father remarks I am too young to discuss the war.
I have heard the talk from Mum's wireless
in the kitchen, my face against the cool Laminex table.

Backseat kids squabble and pinch, tire of *I spy*.
Mum pacifies with promises of Christmas gifts,
seeing Nanna and Pa in Dalmeny. My brother farts.

Sweaty little bodies stick to vinyl seats,
kids doze to the drone of wheels chasing bitumen
and wake to dusk, smells of salty seaweed.

Dawn breaks over grassy dunes and rock pools.
Lazy days, with Mum and Nan, by Mummuga Lake.
Sea sneaks through the inlet, crawls up our sandbar.

Flowing water rolls and rises, melts footprints
away. Our hands hold bright buckets and spades,
summer's sun dips into a blazing horizon –

my child's brain imagines how the rays
illuminate dense jungles of Vietnam –
as bombs and foliage fall, burning flesh.

We find our way home, covered with goose bumps,
a chilling draught in the shadows –
Dad and Pa return with flathead and snapper for tea.

Dragstar

We are on the long dirt track
lined by ghostly Manna gums
whispering stories of the past.

My brother rides his Dragstar
cruising with two friends.
I run, competing with wheels
never to be my own.

Rusty fences and orchards
herald destination dam.
Its surface, dark green lily pads
massed with white and pink flowers.

The boys pedal hard, gain speed
laughter swallowed by distance.
I chase tyre imprints, breathlessly
yell *waaaitt.*

Trudging home embraced by
circles of dusty sunlight
I hear the Dragstar's bell.

Wedding

Two faces,
my sister's open and wide,
ribbon in her hair,
toothy smiles.

Two skinny figures
in long white dresses,
frozen in black and white,
almond-eyed.

Two flower girls, Barb the bride.
I clasp my bouquet with a fist,
sister's hand in a grip,
feet set wide.

1971, Little Mother

Black and white memory, seven, home from school.
Slotted light slips between venetian blind blades.

The lounge is hot and dreamy, phone rings in the kitchen,
bright conversation, muffled talk, long pauses.

White socks stick to harsh wiry carpet as I pace –
stop, eyes focused on woven red wall hanging.

Sweaty hands fold the fabric up the wall, release –
it whirs down, batten hits plaster and bangs sharply,

light drifts over pale blinds, fingers roll, release –
I feel a chill. Mum walks into the room sobbing,

gulping warm air, she blurts, her mother *has died.*
I imagine Nan on the floor, as if fallen from the sky,

arms and legs extended to catch the wind. Her heart still.
Attacked. Mum secrets dreadful pain, Nanna took her life.

In the bathroom I hold her shoulders as they shudder.
Who is going to look after me now? My promise: *I will.*

I cannot breathe, light turns to dark,
the shape of our house begins to change.

Seer

I become wary of people
by the time I turn eight,
locked spaces dark and airless
teach me to appreciate blackness
beyond fear and grief.
A distant voice calms me,
visions of the future
appear like a tv screen,
current world disappears.
Language of all things rumbles
in my ears.
Climb high into trees, feel cloud, touch sky,
descend through drains into the earth,
water flows into my darkness.
The voice inside, *run away from the past*
into the future
through black and white days of construction
I run so fast, my feet barely touch down.

Plants colour our garden, deep purple
and hot pink bells of Mum's fuchsia.
Outside the toy cupboard, stone pot
of Nan's hoya, soft pink and red stamens.
Along the back fence, orange of apricot,
yellow-green of pear, red of nectarine.
Abandoned to darkness
the way out is not with my body.

You appear through a crack of light,
I become silent.

The Mythology Of Life

Dad says 'Cooinda', is an Aboriginal word for happy place. He has bought a block of land on a road to an extinct volcano. Dad's escape from teaching in classrooms, his mission to give children from the suburbs a taste of country air, the intricacies of nature. We are moving to the bush and building a holiday centre. Running conferences, retreats, functions, recreational and educational activities for school camps. Dad will teach orienteering and nature study. How to pan for gemstones in creeks with gold and silver, sapphires and zircons. I am sick with excitement. Hours of swimming, tennis, orienteering and archery. Horse riding and grooming, wagon rides, bush hikes and best of all, campfires and night walks. I am drawn to stars, the sweet earthy smell of dark.

Mt Eirene turned cold thousands of years ago, a crater of fields and farms, not caverns with stalactites as I hankered for adventure. Never discovered any First Nation People. I imagined I would stumble across Clans living the old ways, I could sense their presence, precious spare time spent searching, no tools, no campfires, nothing. Unknown to us at the time I was sitting in class and playing with the Stolen Generations children. Driven out by colonials, travellers who crossed water, faraway landscapes transported on boots, in threads of coats, within hooves of livestock. Their houses and weeds, altered an ancient world. This suffering land became a mother, father, sibling, an extended family to me.

Dad worked three jobs, lecturing cadets at the police academy, coming home in the dark on his motorbike. Working in town, or on the farms, picking and packing spuds, onions and carrots. Driving the trucks to market at three am. Mum worked in town also. Both taught classes occasionally at the local school.

Our Family romanticised Cooinda, cleared it, burnt everything in towering windrows. Every tree felled marked my skin. Trees of genocide, understory became memory, as a single story, split level building rose from exposed red clay. Paddocks and animal pens constructed, aviaries and haysheds. School days began and ended feeding and tending the animals, preparing food in the kitchen. Holidays spent working as leaders, reading to younger children, tending to fowl, rabbit, pig and goat. Serving food and working in the kitchen. Cleaning, cleaning, cleaning.

No-one in my family was the same, after 'Cooinda'.

Nature Teaches The Children

Fence-line, sign: *trespassers prosecuted, dogs shot on sight.* Slip under the wire, dive into the neighbour's dam. Between reeds, small sentient eyes, lithe black scaled body, red belly gleams. Serpent water, shared, cool against my skin, tingling with primal fear. Reptile and human exit opposite ends, soft clay between my toes. Siblings jam mouths and buckets with blackberries. Back under the fence we slide and head home.

Dreamily drawn to water's glassy tinkle, alone I head off where trees grow close, sword grass spills onto the sloping tangled path to the creek. Rocks with prehistoric leaf imprints are scattered about, a partly rotted log spans the water course. My eyes blink as lace-winged insects hover and climb streams of sunlight, maidenhair whispers my name as moss and fern fingers sprout from my limbs. Squirming cold on my leg reveals a pulse of horror, panicked I flick a slimy leech, its bloody mess clots like deep red *Dieldrin* drenched soil on my skin. Dark beetles trail through leaf litter, chant be *brave, be brave*. This world of otherness embraces me.

The recycled weatherboard outdoor dunny has webs attached to timber crossbeams, red stripe along black abdomen draws instant sweat. On rainy nights, wind rises, our flimsy shed iron creaks, young imaginations run wild. Eucalypts almost touch the stars, crash against each other, bark and tough leathery leaves blown free scrape across metal roof, transform our place to a cavern of terror as pounding rain and reckless water consume the world. Our brother waves shadowy arms, roars loudly in the dark, thrilled by our screams, guts wrenched with fear.

Nature, the storm, the wildness in this place, bridled, set loose – like humans, beautiful, terrible.

Picking Grass

Old Sonny was saved from the knackery,
        a wall-eyed stew-ball, loved an ear scratch,
to be hand fed, dragged his back legs.
        Ears turned to my stories as I groomed
him and Kojak the donkey,
        coarse hair the colour of stringy-bark, an unpredictable
bray sounding like despair.
        Alphas: Timmy, black Welsh Mountain pony,
Nicky, chestnut, son of the racehorse Beauty,
        their kicks and bites bruise my body memory.
In the lower paddock, my horse Misty
        the gelding dapple grey, Nicky's half-brother.
Like us kids, all workers,
        pony rides, their job of distinction.
Down the road on agistment was Ricky the stallion.
        By the roadsides after school we picked grass.
Horse paddocks were low, free feed abundant.
        Crouched in umbriferous damp patches of grey-green foliage,
our little hands would eventually ache,
        tearing at succulent stems, filling large woven bags,
my father pressing the contents firmly down.
        Sometimes my mind would stray
into the nearby pine plantation over drifts of rusty needles
        to towering eucalypt forest, bark hanging like scarves.
Spongey black humus and bush alongside
        the creek's overgrown track demanded exploration.
Biting down on soursob stems made us gasp, we giggled,
        mouths pouted, feigning distaste.
Time to turn homeward, as shadows grew long
        my father stacked our hastily filled sacks
onto the tractor dray, we jostled and piled on behind.
        Slowly he drove the Ferguson around the windy roads
a look in his eyes I always observed
        when he was out in the open.

1976, Less Than A Second

climb
ancient pine tree –
a kind of rough love
to juvenile embrace –

leap
a calculated act of bravery–
exiting one dimension
in search of another –

suspended
the entire world goes quiet –
one hundred percent
human child in space –

flight
that Icarus moment –
spirit soars empowered
upon a mighty wind –

grounded
through the bike shed roof –
wood and bone splinter
child finds earth –

Tree Goanna, Lace Monitor

Varanus varius

forked tongue flicks
tastes air senses prey
measures temperature

rough dark reptilian
skin   bands of yellow
spots of cream

stringy bark resident
limbs muscular
wise eyes pierce

i glimpse you
in the hen house
collecting eggs

we were primed
to lie down
when you ran

your claws
could shred flesh
wide open

like that time i cut myself
with the farm knife
blood and strangled silence

In The Scrub

Our neighbour Jock wakes up in the dark, goes out for a leak,
faces the returning bush, flowering banksia, startled wallaby.
Glimmering above, a speckled sky, seams of silver to pluck,
trade for whisky, *International Roast* and food, fuel for the stove.

Bull frogs *plonk*, a deafening chorus.
Is it like years ago... is it like home?

The shed is sparse, he tidies the place, mumbles to himself,
the dark-faced wallaby, echidna burrowing under banksia.
Kids might drop in after school, extra cups by empty sink,
he lights the stove, kettle boils. Frogs fall silent.

Old Jock West was found frozen on the sofa.
I remember the red of his woollen blanket.

Broken Light

A gangly twelve-year-old shuts the gate
beside pale paper-bark of swamp melaleuca.

Thrashing and flicking, a startled copperhead –
flared equine nostrils snort, eyes widen to white.

Sixteen and a half hands rear up on hind legs,
muscle and veins ripple, my Dad high in the saddle.

Dapple grey stallion with the weight of his rider
crashes to the ground, crushes my Father –

his shout, my scream, the broken whinny,
four hooves flailing, a frantic man's push.

Submerged

five thirty morning dive gooseflesh and shivers

winter's water heat shocked from body –

amniotic underworld welcomed silence

grip of pressure upon eyes, ears, nose, muted-mouth –

glide amphibious along blue tiles

sky pulls like a magnet

breaking and splitting

lungs' resisted breath –

feet kick arms stroke plough watery depths

instinct propels me through the surface

fish faced mouth flaps like gills –

thrust into the shattering world of sound –

stroke inhale kick exhale stroke inhale kick

I Was A Bleeder, And Spinner

Our parents had no time for doctors, no belief in sickness –
I tried to hide it up my sleeve, press it into my gumboots,
ate raw garlic on cheese. Staggered off to play netball
and hockey, reeking, to fulfill expectations.
My father, brother and friends made me shudder
as they muttered *boof-head, fat-head, hypochondriac,*
to my child of pain, on days I suffered migraine.

Competed – squeezed my world into a tiny box.
Stumbled, suffering through school – low to high.
Poetry and drama; couldn't keep me off the stage.

I was the family jester, some days sharper than a knife.
Worked my share of family business into dark.
Cooked and served, people left me feeling strange,
outside laughing, insides thrashed and spun, ashamed.
I was bleeding, anaemic and fatigued, couldn't breathe.
Headaches, back pain – acting everything was alright.
Played my ABBA records, dreamed a different life.

Unidentified disease, washed in *Pinetarsol*, smeared in cortisone
I was a child of pain, everything hidden under my itching skin.
Don't let anything out, crack a joke, keep it all within.

Pages

In the evenings, our family read –
dishes wiped and put away,
oats prepared for the morning.
Lamps went on, tv turned off,
our faces illuminated by words.

Books existed the moment I sat up.
Between trees and pages
impenetrable unspoken thoughts.
Our lives shifted location
we sought miracles and mysteries.

Wardrobes filled with classics
studied by aunts, uncles and cousins,
shelves of children's books, poetry
previously owned by grandparents.
My family bound in books by words.

Newspapers read during tea break
piled up in the kitchen
informing us about now, back then.
My tree companions and me
faded into the pages.

Dichotomy

submerged and air-borne
intervening light and dark

between words on the lines
assumed male and female

balancing death with life
acceptance and rejection

sanity and madness
swift and frozen

child between
brother and two sisters

agony and okay
spinning and still

past and present
amid layers of self

never a singular path
merging phases of life

on the outskirts
of consolation and twinge

no end of beginnings
no ending

Millions Of Micro-Organisms In One Drop Of Water

^

Fresh
water laps
the ankles of my
maternal grandmother,
bathes her two daughters,
three sons. Ancestral water
touches them in rivers and creeks,
hydrates them from the dam. Rain falls
over the farm. Briny water rolls down cheeks
at the birth of children, wedding days, as waters
break too soon. Ocean laps the hull of an American
destroyer, Nanna pregnant with my father leaves their
belongings on Pacific Island sand, boards the homebound
vessel. In Seymour they settle. Goulburn River flows around
two daughters and two sons. Children raised alongside banks
where they swim, fish and play. Two families cross paths, my
mother meets my father, our lives sealed by the band of the river,
shaped with the flow of water. Time and river thrashes over granite.
Kayak capsizes, turbulence sucks me below willows, relinquished to
yellowy depths, liquid encompasses me, consumes me with language.
Forgetting the perfumes of home I sink into time, the flow. Arms rip
body to the surface. Gasping, my eyes open to a blue sky applied with
perfection. Araucaria bidwillii shelters stocky seedling, trees reveal a
sacred story, sun shines through droplets of rain, in sepia the flowing
river speaks a language water knows, now I know. Thin talk racing
past pebbles, resonant comments to embankment hollow, dialects
of rock fall, gnarled roots within silent eddies. Choral outpourings
mist upwards, catch The Fremantle Doctor, Southerly Buster.
Bellowing at watery junctions, poetic whispers, waterfall's
chant, chatter of lagoon, river deltas humming to
great oceans. Our worldly vernacular of aqua
sings with BunyaBunya and the millions
of micro-organisms sprung
from one droplet
of water.

On Eildon Weir

river water flows
pools and laps
sounds bring relief
our canoe drifts
oars dip and drip
water of summer

into the weir we glide
weave past skeletal trees
defined by white light
under infinite blue sky

teenage outlines
ash against straw
coloured hills
over ripples voices skip
our laughter
returns and circles

we had no idea
of what was to come

One Of Auntie's 'Queer Fish'

I'm the child who learnt to explore, run and climb,
alongside Pippy Longstocking, I play outside,
hide away from the hungry looks of men,
eyes sliding all over our skin, a warning
sign followed by hands, and other things.

My sisters craved reassurance, potent, feminine,
wore make-up, attracted attention,
dressed in fashion with hemline ascension,
flashing wide eyes, drinking and smoking.
Boyfriends driving fast, in hotted-up cars.
For this game, I built armour and spear.

On the outskirts of the football throng
a quiet watcher observing the different few,
mean kids huddled, plotting someone's misery.
Older kids with sex on their minds,
all of us outcasts searching for sameness.

Underaged smokers and tokers, the sniffers.
Slurred speech from innocent secret chuggers
Des and Rocky in their baggy jeans.
Hiding behind buildings and embankments
where the western sun would glare
through needle leaves of deep green pines.

Under Winter's Shadow

Childhood was built around sport, Dad's football ruled.
Huge ovals, fragments of churned mud and grass,
cold steel tubular rails the powerful circular divide.
Cars parked like haphazard bricks of colour
mortared into the yellow sandy rutted roads.
Canteen oozed tomato sauce, hot pies, pasties and sausage rolls.
Rainbows of lollies stacked in boxes like teeth in a rotting smile.

Collective emotions, rise and fall, hum and rumble builds
into a human storm, fades to eerie quiet, speckled with the call
and response of possession-focused players. Leather on leather
as boot meets ball, *thunk* of colliding bodies and footfall.
Horns jubilantly toot as ball sails between goal posts. Scrape
then clunk, large metal numbers change on the score board.

Half time trumpet call, barley water and mountains of sliced orange.
I watch the boys pass their pet footballs, pretending
to be their favourite players, eyes distant in admiration.
Huddles of plain and striped guernseys, men slurp and spit,
mumble and bellow, look down, shameful silence as coach riles
them up, rails them down. Match restarts to piercing eyes, grinding jaws,
mouths working guttural sounds, the cheer.

Women huddle over bags of wool crocheting blankets, toddlers
at their feet, future footballers squirm and crawl, eat discarded
cigarettes and beer drenched soil, older siblings sneak alcoholic dregs.
Adults glare at the opposition, engrossed in the game, ordinary daily
faces morphed into a singular creature, be it a glorious winner
or a grudging fistful loser. Siren ends the game with a mighty roar,
home-crowd swarms onto the ground, kicking balls.

Two streams of men jog into the clubhouse, wet wool and mud,
Deep Heat, steam and sweat, studs on their boots echo of horse hooves.
Children wander into rowdy change rooms, sing the team song,
sent out in liniment scuffles, pungent menthol permeates the cool air.
Adolescents share stolen kisses between parked cars
as I search for my siblings under winter's shadow of descending dark.

Cancer Is Not Only A Constellation

She painted birds, sewed dresses, all the latest fashion. I was grateful to receive woolly tartan trousers. Her family gave me a photo book on baby animals. She commented my face was as cheeky as the young otter, I liked that. The left side of Auntie Gee's face sagged after the stroke, quietly she explained to me that inside her head was an inoperable brain tumour, the size of an orange.
Artists with children die.

He taught me to play chess, while listening to Dark Side of the Moon and Otis Redding. The proud father of my favourite baby cousin. Adults' hushed whispers about bone marrow donation, while I read my 1979 *Peanuts* annual, led me to ask if my own marrow could help. Moles excised from Uncle Ray's back, wounds refused to heal, bones devoured by leukemia. An anaesthetist's sleep, impossible to wake from.
Even doctors die.

Nan had us for roast on Sundays. She loved Dickens, gave me *Oliver Twist, Great Expectations*, her copy purchased from and titled, *The Old Curiosity Shop*. Her favourite was *David Copperfield*. She loved cats, but settled for a potted Anthurium. When Nanna came to stay, gone was the jar of sweets on the mantle, we had to care for her. She lost her hair, wore a wig. Her working life dedicated to bringing life into the world twisted by loss, her own shortened life.
Midwives die too.

Walking home from the school bus on my fifteenth birthday Mum passed me in the car, stopped, wound down the window. I could tell by her face Ray had died. No cake, no candles. Soon after, Gee passed away, followed by Nanna. Few explanations. Each of our satellites drifted further into the galaxy. So began a life of orbits in dark matter.

Cancer in the constellation of Cancer, glimmers of life in starlight, plucked away in crab claws.

(Missing)

I disappeared the day my brother shut me in the toy cupboard,
screams and sobs ended in sleep between boxes and darkness.

In my teens I found comfort as I climbed into tight places
closed the door, heard people call, never answered, just vanished.

My sister's innocence, seduced by some smart-assed guy with wheels,
corner shadows darkened, car door slammed and she was gone.

Parents out, planned winter party, we waited, listening to 3XY up loud
Split Enz, Aussie Crawl, Blondie sang *Atomic*, our friends didn't arrive.

Rang mates, hospitals, cops. Motorbike smash outside Emerald.
Sister's boyfriend in intensive care, clinging to life. Pink Floyd.

Best friend pillion, no helmet, ventilated, comatose, in Dandenong
Hospital. One blink yes, two no. *Ashes to Ashes*, remained locked in.

Youth lost to jagged experience. People searched, called and called –
missing boy from a nearby town, part of us, disappeared, forever.

1980s, Under Pressure

No entry on the door of my room full of books.
Chatty flamboyant exterior cloaks a brooding poet
in colour. *Brass in Pocket*, to *Comfortably Numb.*
Barometric mood hits a false high with a tap of tension.

Responsible, negotiator, peacemaker, sisters' chaperone –
to movies like *The Shining* which terrified me. Kids pashing
made me squirm, remained aloof as the alcohol flowed.
'Long story short, I lost my mind', started drinking.

People often mistook me for a boy or a girl, didn't identify
as a boy, nor a girl; gone was ABBA, I'm 'Rebel, Rebel'.
Boys, disloyal and mean, waged war after war –
Girls betrayed me in search of boys and glamour.

The travelling faith-makers preyed on my mother,
left her with their bible and *The Watchtower* magazines.
She placed them on my desk, open to passages,
I fill with self-hatred, homophobia.

I went riding with Norris on his KZ1300 motorbike,
the wind, the freedom, we sped around twisted roads.
Didn't want his romance, just wanted friendship,
all that pain on his face, confusion stifled inside.

Fragments Of Clay Pigeon Day

From the desk
in my room
I hear:
snap, load
click, release
crack of gunshot
multiple parts
of clay pigeon
explode out over dense scrub.
The jovial atmosphere
between the men, slaps on backs
the boy takes a cartridge, loads
snap, click, crack. Thunderous echo.
My poetry
punctuated
in all the wrong places.

Weight And Guilt

I ask myself to be –
the rock, the sand, the minerals, the soil,
the lichen, the ferns, the grasses, the trees, algae.
The rain, the river, the lakes, the creatures.
I ask myself to be –
chemist, astrophysicist, geologist, botanist, biologist,
painter, sculptor, photographer, philosopher, poet.
I ask myself to be
blind and the eyes that see –
to burn, to reflect, to breathe, to speak,
to write of the ocean that rises, retracts, surges,
of land cracked open, pushed up, subsiding,
washed over by sea.
I ask myself
to be –

I Say Dad…

My father was Ulysses, Achilles,
Hector, Priam.
My father was the golden wedge-tailed eagle,
a hunter, never the hunted.

My father was Superman,
The Incredible Hulk, Mr Universe.
My father was a boxer, footballer,
a champion sportsman.
An educator, jack of all trades.
He knew how to live from the land.

My father was a man's man.
A horse whisperer, colt breaker.
A charmer, generous and giving.

My father was a chameleon
giving from places already taken.
Expectation and discipline
filling us with fear.

Knives And Sibling Rivalry

i.
Thump,
I grip my brother's tape-deck.
Two torsion wires vibrate,
then twang.

Woosh shhhh.
Orange rubber
bouncer ball deflates.
Glint of steel,
flicker of madness.
I am twelve,
my brother fourteen.

ii.
Shouting over the table.
We have forgotten
what was said.
His steak-knife
strikes just below
my jugular notch.

Sisters' mouths
open.
Red splashes
over stunned
silence.
I am fifteen,
he is seventeen.

Sister, Brother, Identity

Children declared *uncivilised,* fighting and spitting in the wild,
Presbyterian faith left behind, a brother with guns and knives,
we were fighting for our lives.

Dumbing down our intellects, fighting for status
outside the paradigm of a strict upbringing.

Sisters' secrets protected, my queerness buried in books.
Our brother on sporting highs and arrogant weekend bashings,
trying to hide his other side, love of art and Rocky Horror,
Frank-n-Furter in fish-net stockings.

Mum rode pillion on his bike to Belgrave for art classes.
Late at night in her studio of freshly varnished panelling,
she painted a more colourful life. We craved her love and mothering.
Dad sulked when off the footy field. They argued, always working.
My brother shone, jewel in the town, their handsome champion.

He could be cruel, flashing a flick-blade knife, sisters' screams of futility.
He crossed a line to petty crime with footy mates on weekends,
fun was blowing up a phone box, the *Hot Line's*
scent of dynamite attracted police attention.

This wasn't the envisaged ride our young family embarked on,
wheels off, dragging behind.

Silverback father, chest beating, wounded and suffering,
sharp teeth bloody and sneering. I had read they eat their offspring.
His glare and cynicism crippling,
our tears and humiliation welled with the thrashings.

Volunteered in the library, read every volume given.
In my locker, Salinger's silver books, a bottle of Johnny Walker.
Skipped class, got detention, took it out on the page,
raged on the stage, obsessed with Plath and Dylan Thomas.

On his last motorbike ride my brother crashed, instantly died.
I survived, angry and on fire, fighting against everything.
Knew it should have been me.

Post Mortem

I grieve in a cold mountain river.
Water swirls around my body,
my stony life in melted snow –
tastes like time beginning.

Water swirls around my body,
as rain falls from wild leaves –
a taste of time beginning,
pushing up with the high country.

As rain falls from wild leaves,
a plump and jovial naked babe
is pushed out of the high country,
seasoned with memory of trees.

Once a plump and jovial babe,
this stony life is melted snow,
seasons and memories of trees.
I grieve in a cold mountain river.

At The Crematorium, 1981

A throat of blue-red flames roared
as the shiny metal door opened wide.
Nanna, Dad's mother, in her coffin
glided inch by inch into the fire.

At her funeral the priest seemed to shed
more tears than I could understand.
During the wake, my cousin clasped
her hands around my neck, squeezed.
Spluttering I pulled away, her raw pain,
her mum's recent death. My red face.

Two Earth orbits around the sun.
A door yawns, a 'Mt Doom' glow.
My brother's youthful carapace
tracks into the blazing interior.

The mid-field service, footy oval farewell,
four hundred mourners left in our wake.
Six of us stand rigid, red eyes fixed.
His life disappears into the furnace.
Within me old death embers flare
as the crematorium's steel door snaps shut.

The Marauders

Three wild dogs attacked
the gelding dapple grey,
biting and ripping,
on a dark windy day.
I raced to the house
found my brother's gun –
loaded, pulled the trigger,
out the bullet spun.

Snarl became yelp
as slug made its mark,
I felt remorse
for my defensive part.
When wracked by fear
I took to the gun –
in the cur's defeat
I hadn't won.

In both hands
a wood and metal gun,
an open shaft,
gelding on the run.
A shot for life
in a field of death –
lead pellets and hair
on wild dog's breath.

Time Traveller

for a moment everything is sliding
my head is shifting back in time
as my body wrenches forward
brain caught between trains
I sense I'm falling down
in opposite directions
this punishment
my weakness
I force myself to focus
steel plates slide back and forth
within a still moment I project forward
one last intention imprinted in my mind

Cracks

I wandered Sherbrooke Forest
in the gloom of winter –
slept in soft leaf litter
below a rhododendron shelter.
Poor reports from school,
felt completely flawed –
tangled in life's pattern,
unable to find a way home.
My grieving family trapped
in pure survival and struggle, no energy
to love, my sorrow too much trouble.
Free to roam among trees, no questions
asked by bark or stone –
a place for all, kids hanging out
around warmth of fire, cow-eyed
red-faced, wistful for love.
Some disappeared, others died –
I curled up with moss and owl.

Exit Stage Left

The lights we set streamed orange. The lines learnt were in the wrong places. You've gone, a lost cause. It was clear from the phone call that night. The ten-month mark, a curse. Ten, the day of my birth, a number tied to your indifference. You sixteen, me seventeen, life wrung out, corrupted. Knife fragments pierce my body, slash at sensitive flesh. How could such bliss turn into stench and darkness, agony and anger? No sharing with friends the latest crush, dreams of love, or moments of heartbreak, an existence hiding beneath rock, toadstool, under a boot. Skylab fallen to Earth. Soft fruit, ravaged by the sun. Loss has left me loveless, emotionless, sexually diffused. A Grim Reaper's bowling ball casualty. Condemned to shameful silence, I shave my head, pick at sores, make more, slam fists into walls, bleed tears from unseeing eyes. No smile, no celebration, no commiseration, our secret destruction. Curtain call, exit stage left.

Once we lay together
and for all its confusion,
we loved each other.

Desire

It's gone to sleep
after the violent end
and confusing beginning.
We shivered and shuddered
with excitement and fear
of the unknown.
How longing
would linger
our breath of lust
catapulting sparks
into evening skies
lit up dawn's
horizon like
a wild fire.
She would
drive me
for miles
only to
feed me
knives
and
humiliation.

Following Ouroboros

I studied nature with my feet in moss,
knees on earth, nose to the breeze,
summer oils, musk in humus.
Through sickness and health
hands in rich soil,
eyes on the detail,
ears turned to leaf rustle,
branch snap, bird call.
I vibrated as the world vibrated,
drank from minerally mountain streams,
relished creamy fresh dew.
Stroked grass heads along pathways
to ancient sandy beaches,
floated on water's surface
tasting salt, blandness of wind.
Lying in the dunes upon Banksia leaf litter
I listened to animal conversations at night.
Stars burned bright, then faded
under the shadow of human light.

My Mother Through Flames, Ash Wednesday 1983

the evacuation of kids staying at the school camp in Gembrook

The phone call comes as sleep claws, *evacuate, get the kids out now.* Burnt eucalyptus oil and smoke fill the air. Billowing orange and red cloud rain gentle flecks of ash. Roaring fills our ears and flames begin to surround us. Once the bus leaves, Mum, my young sisters and I, climb into the Triumph Stag, full of apprehension we leave Dad and drive into the fire. The blaze is rampant on both sides of the narrow road. Flames gnash high above the car, I am bolstered with clarity and calm as I navigate us through blinding smoke, encourage mum to keep going, to focus. We hit the bitumen, the road widens.

Norm's school bus, full of young kids on camp, is parked on the football oval. In the club rooms the local women are making sandwiches, tea and coffee, for evacuees and fireys. From the canteen we watch my mother arguing with a city motorbike cop sent to escort the children back to desperate parents. We have radioed Brian the fire chief, to come and sort things out. I think about Dad, back home fighting the flames to save our house, the holiday centre. Communications down.

Elocution and deportment bristle against condescension. Duty to protect the kids strains in her rising soprano voice, *I'm sorry, the fire chief releases the bus, not you.* Ember warpaint is smudged across her cheeks, salt and pepper hair tidy, in spite of a night on the bus. Her sapphire kaftan with swirls of white, billows in the wind. The blow-in cop stamps, commands Norm to proceed. He looks towards Mum, her green eyes gleam, as ignition turns, engine grunts then purrs. Motorcycle cop straddles bike, fastens his helmet.

Mum throws herself in front of chrome grille and looming wheels. *Over my dead body.* The Clash belt out, *Rock the Casbah.* Brian approaches the motorbike and pulls the keys from the ignition.

Soft Fruit

Raspberries didn't always come in plastic punnets. Pinkish pixel villages, bleeding at the slightest pressure. Raspberries blast my tastebuds. Red juice runs along blemished fingers into a ravenous mouth, a flash and snare of tangled canes in the valley.

Half adult, half teen, saving for escape to Sydney. Thorny stems terrorised tender fingers picking at high speed over Monbulk red soil. Raspberries were the shape of me, aggregated and hollow inside. *Sweet Dreams* of that big harbour city.

Standing at the Manly wharf pay phones, in a shroud of cigarette smoke and salt, pleas for me to return to Melbourne were met with stunned-fish silence. HSC results ringing in my ears, flashes of sweat, wall of black in my skull, blank exam papers. The wound stains me still.

First love's taste of ending, death, wildfires, Mum and Dad filing for divorce. Empty, all my words stolen. Water slapped red-gum pylons; deep blue waves carried my ferry to Circular Quay. Displaced, I boarded the fast train to Taree, a ballast of secrets inside me.

Drank Bundy OP in the pub, staggered to the Manning River, muddy currents spun and swirled, their destination a mystery. I searched for a way to tell my childhood friend I'm queer. Taree's humid air a thick scent of frangipani, berry-pink blooms covered the streets to her share house.

Outside the record store a Eurythmics poster, Annie's bright lips. At the greengrocer in shallow wooden trays – raspberries and me with no money left to pay.

Leaving Childhood

Like a cement block wall with dodgy foundations, I hit the age my brother was when he died. Our large house emptier than ever before. Crinoline curtains, peacock blue shagpile tired and worn from years of camp kid foot traffic. Ghostly dormitories echoed chattering youth, fading in and out of the unexpected vacancy. Orange shower cubicles shimmered in muted afternoon light. Mum's fear the Health Inspector would close us down, demanded obsessive hygiene. I will never scrub urinals again.

Dad had been indiscreet, flirting, *carrying on.* Mum wasn't having it, went west, ended up stuck in Port Hedland with a cyclone. Couldn't escape turbulence, no matter where she went. Her new house was in town. Dad and I were left behind, wandering the living spaces, two spectres drifting in at night from our miserable drinking sessions. Found camaraderie in poverty and hunger. Women had broken our hearts, crushed our egos. The great man fractured, no need for fear or to prove myself. He'd been dumped. So had I. It was after Ash Wednesday, someone crossed out Gembrook and scribbled *separation city* onto the sign.

The house was empty. Sold to new owners. Gone was the bustle of family, staff, children, students and teachers. The yearly screening of *My Fair Lady.* Our bright dreams embedded in charcoal and dust. The last day, a hive of cooperation. Everything packed, a convoy of vehicles drove away. Leaving childhood, the land that fed me, loved me. No home to go to. I cracked like a burnt out stringybark, splintered and crashed to the ground.

Outsider

i.

No home, broken family.
My story nothing new,
no place to be free
from the layer of scum
judgement placed on me.

No home,
punch me to a pulp –
I won't hate you
for hating me.

No home,
your eyes meet mine
look away.
I don't feel the difference
you clearly do,
your face says it all –
not my place.

ii.

Spinning in a siren's whirlwind,
not sure which box to tick.
Spinning in a new world double flush,
struggling to climb out of the closet
someone pushed into the space
outside the last closet I stepped through.

Dog's Life

Mum's greatest love didn't last,
all divorce and carnage,
broken foundations, our past dragged
me down, twice she kicked me out.

All love comes at a price,
lesson learned, you paid big to stay,
even in places hearts didn't touch.
Lying down with dogs,

Mum declared, *you will get up with fleas*
but I found I could make my mark,
run wild, tongue lolling in scented streets,
roll and scratch in mountain dirt.

I knew where I stood among the mange
and scars, the jostle of pack and fang bite.
Padding on all fours into the night.
I learned to howl at the moon.

Invert

Radcliffe what have you left me?
A dose of sacrificial gallantry.
I know so well your loneliness.
This fire inside fuelled by a Robin
Morgan 'monster', my anthology
of American lesbian poets.
We pierce the eyes of that opposite gaze.

For her, my tits upright
pouting with bad attitude,
my spiked hair scraping
tender thighs on the way
to places my tongue
should never mention.

Butch or femme,
cram me into lesbian skin.
Pat, line up the bar.
I'm going to Richmond
yeah, women's night at the Kingston.
Hell, I am full of life,
ready to explore every
fucking centimetre of it.

Passion, Powder And Sting

Hecate and Rena
dark and light.
Intrigued and unsure
I'm drawn to their fire,
punk attitude, spiked hair.
Forces of rage and rejection
burn behind blue and brown eyes.

Pupils set. Spoons and white
powder to the flame.
Patti Smith blares
down the hallway
out the open door
over the valley.
Banshees dance,
sound like horses
merging with the hallway.

Two women possessed
by their passion to love
and be loved.
Springs entwined
bursting, high tension
escapes.

Red satin sheets
thrashed
into crumpled
emptiness.

Au Pair

I flew west
wearing Gabrielle's
black boots,
Rena's leather shirt.
Drunk and obtuse.

Arrived in Perth
with a Mohawk's head,
out and confused,
blood pumping dread.

On the Melbourne bus
the very next day.
Children's hesitant hands
waved me away.

Wearing unwashed jeans,
Joanne's studded belt,
I bear the great divide,
miles of red desert
deepen the wound inside

The Shadow Hunters

On the streets when I walk
two shadows fall
my androgynous soul
sprouts ambivalence from the core
gender bender for sure
wherever I walk
two shadows on the floor

I hang out with junkies
drag queens and dykes
hookers and outcasts
punks in the night.

I never stay long, always on the run
from despair, old scars,
words jangled in the thrum.
Looking for answers, lost in the wind
searching for love, no one will give.

On the streets when I walk,

hey poofter, punk, you dyke!
we'll catch you, we'll cut you,
nail your soul to a wall...

into a dark pool of blood
my two shadows fall –

but I rise and I swipe my light from their hands
I yell I run and I roar.
I am what I am
Fuck you all

Vigilance Splits The Sonnet

knowing what happens to
girls
I learned to walk like a
boy
knowing what happens to
girls
I spoke with a deeper
voice
knowing what happens to
girls
I carried a knife at
night
knowing what happens to
girls
I taught my arms and legs to
strike
knowing what happens to
women
walking the street
alone
knowing what happens to
women
hanging out at
home
knowing what happens to
women
I trained white fists to
fight

Baby Dyke

Not long left *Monnie* High, school poet laureate two years in a row, wild inside, art, theatre and words pumping through my sharp, eager brain. Trying to earn some coin, broke in a *recession we had to have.* I am urns of penniless poetry, Keats and Ern Malley, the fake and fraud, the genuine, searching for love, to be, to be. I am at Heide, ghosting Sunday Reid and the Heart garden, Bert and Ned, some forty years before they spilled paint for the country. War a constant drip of water running down our psyche, the walls at the Victorian gallery, some stolen Picasso, grimy dark streets in Fitzroy. Find me in bookshops like The Shrew, the Theosophical. Collingwood Town Hall women's dances, spiked drinks, fighting back like a wild cat. St Kilda pubs in black punk-goth revolution, crazy for Siouxsie Sioux. The Palais '84 front row for The Cure. I am protesting, writing political statements on walls with women, wild women, mountain women, voices yelling out into the night getting arrested for bloody paint on war memorials. No nuclear missiles. No more murder or rape. We want peace. I am *baby dyke,* that *fucking lesbian with the smart mouth*, can't handle my drink, far from home, curious in the city, *too nice for the city*, knowing fear, but unafraid, hanging with friends at The Prince of Wales, the brothel; make me bad, make me shine. Cops on the job, cops on the job letting me go, got the gift of the gab. Raids in the rush of blood city, the Australia Hotel, gay bar in the city, no women's loos, pissing standing up and laughing it out. Barry and Buddha's city loft full of people, making free phone calls, talking about this thing called AIDS, watching friends share the needle. I am some Upwey share house down the road from Fred Williams' old place. Upstairs downstairs grotto share house, close to the half-way house, living on baked potato. Looking for work with jail birds, Spider and Polly, the strugglers, day-work on building sites, cleaning bricks for some cash, some coin for petrol to drive the VW beetle down to town. Looking for love, same-same love. I am 19, I have a mountain inside.

Home Invasion

Van pulls up in moonlight, man says he has a gun,

bangs on the windows, rumbles, yells, *run*.

Man crashes through the door, face distorted with hate.

My chest pounds in moonlight, darting terror eyes.

Hide from stalking car lights, sudden slamming doors.

Jelly legs in the half dark, dirt and panic fill my nose.

Wild reflections in moonlight on the phone-box glass.

Wake weighted, heavy footsteps, erase experience.

Throw on my long overcoat, collar flipped.

Drive to work, check side streets in hidden suburbs.

Pull my socks up, gut writhes, transform and smile,

gag, taste rotten secrets, feel control slide

as day slips to night. Smell, touch and taste – fear.

Jockey Of The Night

i. Him, ii. Her, iii. Me

i.

He ignored the restraining order. Rode night
shift at shopping centre malls, sweeping up butts
and dust of civilization, frisking dump masters for
the discarded. Fallen equine racer, rider with a twisted
hand, scarred wrists map some past effort to take his life.
Phone call harassment, threatened us with his gun, hired a thug
to stalk me, to rearrange my face.

ii.

My partner was older, great sense of humor,
shimmy in her eyes, cascading smile. Around her
kids she was a lioness. Couldn't sleep at night without
a light, knew the touch of bikie brutal violence. No police
intervention, fear of repercussion. Broken families entwined,
children the bind, anxiety and fear ceases, his heart full of heroin.

iii.

Tried to shield the kids from this adult war.
Her youngest had said to me, *you're my hero.*
Youthful, I wanted to fix things, fortify our family.
A high price for complicated life, seduction of love shatters
something in each of us. Years of intimidation, survived scorched
and strung out. Wild cat bagged under water, fought back, slit the sack,
gave the bricks back, walked away aged, nothing left, nobody's hero.

Colours We Wear

Feminism
battered and blue
I rise for you.

Equality
I open the cast iron
door of history
for you.

Release
the scold's bridle,
sisters speak
we believe you.

Will steps be taken
to stop the violence?
Do hands dare to hold fast
in unification?

Do stolen lives
give us strength
to outstare our
rabbit-in-spotlight fear?

The gunshot is near,
this time
I won't run.

Oh My Goddess

Venus de Milo
is armless –
best call in an army
of artists
to reconstruct –

pristine beauty
deformed
to reform us?
perhaps absent arms
set into stone
warn us –

One Night At The Glasshouse

I gauge, hold my own, *don't yield,*
linger at the edge of the crowd. Catch snippets
of conversation, note hands clutching stubbies,
fingers pick at labels; eyes regard the pool table.
Cool performance characters, China doll faces,
black peaked leather caps, whips, legs in chaps.
Beneath long jackets, chains around necks and straps
support naked breasts. Solid black boots tap.
The stage set '90s techno beat, pumping.

Conversation is achingly shallow, this party all show –
what makes them tick beneath pout and exhibition?
Tension of desire, danger, pheromones heighten.
Who can you trust? Everyone wants something
alarm bells tell me it's everything I am.
Who can you trust? Everyone could be Judas, Brutus.
Enemies in sameness, cloaked in different shades.
Enticed by curiosity, I could almost sell my soul.

On the margins, whisky followed by VB
awkwardness makes me wonder if I belong.
My game comes up, moving with a staged swagger
I retort and slash, a rogue's razor tongue,
pocket balls with a hustler's skill.
My presence in their bar raw and real
cue point to marvellous masquerade,
banter and bravado hang in the air
on bass notes, swirls of cigarette smoke.

We Are The Real Deal Of Human Touch

I met her through Chrissie, matchmaking,
at *Cuttersmith*, trams clattering along Brunswick.
One winter night leaving The Glasshouse,
we embraced, our belt buckles hooked,
untangling the lock fingers flutter, laughter.

A yellow Super-Bug had caught my eye.
When I saw her VW key, I knew it was a sign.
She was won over with my Beetle knowledge,
pulling levers, vents opened to a gush of heat.
Sunflowers adorned the dash, a fusion of warmth.

We walked for hours along St Kilda beach,
gazed at delectable cakes on Acland Street.
Revisited childhood songs from *Let's Sing*.
Possessions stuffed into a tiny Northcote flat.
Slowly unpeeled our lives the light and dark.

Waking Up In Adelaide

I am sailing to the beach straight down Anzac Highway,
no angel gear for this flat road, the lapis lazuli gulf
sings like mermaids and shimmers like snapper scales.
We laugh at the big wide streets, hardly any cars.
Zero cigarette butts and hypodermics in the sand.
Stone cottages and bungalows dwarfed by seldom
cloudy sky, planes soar on a flightpath high.
Thermometer red, rises like the blush of a newborn.
After 29 years in Melbourne, I shift to Adelaide,
my partner's home. Buzz cuts and a whole new scene.
Weathered nursery owners ask, *why'd you move?*
No work here. Under this coruscating sky, gardens are dry.
Hey laddie ain't no work anywhere, old timers sigh,
look me in the eye. I smile at the white blue sky.

We rent a railway cottage up Bridgewater way,
sense spirit here, feel it in my chest, an old woman
tells me about song lines, stolen land's memory,
I believe her, hear voices, a recognisable sadness.
Out back stands an enormous ash tree, freight train
shakes the roots, iron squeals shuddering the leaves.
I think of Jeffery Smart. A cloak drops, dark silence.
Blackened scars from Ash Wednesday mar eucalypts
across the railway cutting, a hot breeze rises.
Icing blue lace cap hydrangeas thrive by the shed,
beauty's cycle unbroken in fifty years of neglect.
Hey laddie ain't no work, why'd ya come so far?
Came to start again, but sorrow is a wound carried
within. Braced, I become the steel of locomotive wheels.

When Sky Swallows The City

I come down in blue
droplets of rain
streaks of felted cloud
grey skies turn black
sink into green.

I come down in blue
festival face paint
river red gum grins
gloved fingers reach
towards nightfall.

I come down in blue
eyes of laughter
stage a banquet of
sunshine to light
up your solitude.

I come down in blue
denim overalls fix
the leaking faucet
hang the back door
on brass hinges.

I come down in blue
cascades of water
your lover again
on this ocean
of winter.

Gardener

Our garden wakes me at five am.
I throw back the covers,
pull on overalls,
plant feet into steel-cap boots,
press hands into leather gloves.
Heart soars with abundant love
beaming from the garden.

Black hound by my side
I sweep around plot and space,
listen to a symphony of chatter
from plants, insects and birds.
Eternally an apprentice.
My grateful lungs fill
with the newborn smell
of morning.

Tree Of The Dead

Death
spared me to suffer,
question, to contemplate
and wait. The brush of *her* cheek
daily, leaves parts of me dying as *she*
winks at me. Lost opportunities of the
dead haunt me. I am worn from experience,
staring into a wound, *her* doing, each recent
loss seeded into the forest of death. Teenagers
obsessed with Janis, Jimmy and Marilyn. Brain
tumour, hanging, leukemia, bowel cancer. Death
of body, locked in spirit. My brother's death, metal
scrapes metal and flesh. Death of our family. Death
of nature, bush, animals, trees charred. Death of
Macbeth, no solace in the classroom. Death of
childhood. Dieldrin-poisoned ground, death
of a town. *Death's* staff kept knocking,
suicide, overdose, hanging,
drowning
Clot,
ends
life.
why?
There
will
always be an answer
from a chameleon's mouth.

Sorrow Of The Sea

Long brown weed piles hide her possessions in a valley of flattened sand. Knit purl, knit purl, along Merricks beach, crustaceans spun into plastic bags, coarsely woven seagrass, woolly rows waiting for waves to cast off to the sea.

Shaggy dog
patiently stands guard,
night fall.

A mourning tide has washed her gently ashore. Rolling foam rises with salty buoyancy through splayed toes, fingers, reaching an absent husband, too long in the afterlife. *Is there an afterlife?* This ocean will always be here, has touched the flesh of millions who have perished. Gives life to billions who live still.

She took her life
into the arms of an amniotic sea
at dawn

Advice To Self

When the storm rages, write the wind, write the thunder, write the rain that falls on broken twisted branches, write the sea rising and crashing over the land, write the storm. Write pain, write things you cannot right, write of rope, knots, of pills, the battle of will. Reinvent yourself, walk up words like a ladder.

Write the hollow ache eroded by wind, silence that gnaws, write the outside, look beyond, reflect the image inside the glass, write the tears, write the rage, write a change, keep writing until you arrive.

Loneliness

Noun 2. (of place) Remote, isolated

Grief drags me down, deep into the ground,
she took her life, left me spluttering,
years of surviving, unravelling, drowning.

Humpty dumpty had a great fall

Sexism, racism, plebiscite,
did I have to end up here, vacant and queer?
Childless, judged and rejected, political pip,
spat out, cast adrift.

Jack fell down and broke his crown and Jill came tumbling after

No queer community, life's lost quality,
surrounded with mortar and stone,
feeling unloved, alone.
Drowning in a divided suburbia.

everywhere that Mary went, the lamb was sure to go

Without greeting
people pass my door,
build high metal fences.

a tissue a tissue, we all fall down

Against the invisible, the un-named,
we are defenceless.
Our country is leaderless.

when the bough breaks...

Lifespan Of The Mad Hag

Mad youth full of life
Madly pluck and suck desire
Mad myriad of *normal*
Mad cow bellowing at the sky

Mad witch on drink
Mad broomsticks clad with thorns
Mad spells and voodoo
Madly cling to the brink

Mad injured hag
Madness in chains
Mad for humus
Mad for the wilds

Madness seeded into fur
Mad bad animal
Mad bird of the night
Mad hag in flight.

I Say Dad, II

My father is a lone man with acres of land.
As the things he loves disappear,
Dad becomes a brooding man.
His ankle joints surgically fused with metal
leave a slowly rusting man.
As the strokes hit and maim,
I see a more determined man.

On the veranda he sits, old dog by his side,
instant coffee in hand,
contemplating all that has passed,
in the company of Mount Oberon.

Mum Says 'Gay Is Good'

Mum learnt to say
Gay is good,
when she could let go of the wish for another son-in-law
and grandchildren from her first daughter.

When she saw I was happy.

Mum learnt to say
Gay is good to her colleagues,
when she was the lone volunteer to care for the new client
who had AIDS.

Plebiscite

November 14, 2017

If you were to love me as I love you
would it be true love?
If your *heart skipped a beat* as we passed on the street
is it true, actual love?
I caught that smile, as your eyes lingered on mine.
My heart soared when your words assured, requited love.

Some think *it's a pity, two girls so pretty*
can find true love. I think it's crazy how it divides
a city, this rush of opinion, a hateful flood.
Two happy souls, not hurting, nor preaching,
just living and giving. Why the heavy thud?

So love is political, what's gender, what's racial,
it's not logical or communal, it hurts.
There's a suicide rise, deep darkness inside,
other people decide, judge and deride, our purity,
our pride, our tired turning of the cheek,
no person is an island, yet we are marooned.

Perfect Nature

Sprays of finite mist
touch softly, soak all surfaces,
as letters form words.
An aria of condensed vapour,
brings life to mosses. Fine roots
grind soil from rock,
delicate antennae calculate
spores of reproduction.
Numbered sky droplets,
nature's perfect structures,
came long before letters,
never strangers to a big bang.

Wooded smell of forest,
shrouded trees under silver veils,
showers of sweet water
absorbed into pores.
Hymns of leafy surfaces,
rough trunks, alluvial soil,
queer light embraces place.

Great feather entwined flocks soar,
drag clouds, muscle and tendon
drive wings, create the wind.
Low vibrato voices rise above steam,
beaks open, their song of the world
enters my ears.

Lost Language

Lost in limited vocabulary, words meanings forgotten.
Articulation strangled, memory fractured, vanishing.
I recall portraits on the walls, young sisters painted in oils,
tribal grass skirts, shields and hunting spears.

Out here in the garden, mosquitos hone in, pierce flesh.
I itch and scratch, slap shadows, actions familiar to every
human being. My only connection, insect, white sky.
Past threads whisper, drift through my jangling mind.

Discarded truth lies beneath layers of ideas, shed skin, clothing.
My heart beats in a rib cage jail, heavy hardened muscle.
Raised in a carnivore's den, bones stewed and strewn.
Trained to defy illness, the natural world somersaults.

Swallow sentient voices sound, light and matter,
thoughts fail to connect with words. Everything we were,
first hand stories, swept away, written into one language.
I stand on the ledge of my history, scratch and weep.

I Felt No Pain While Sleeping

Curb the sorrow for my loathsome disease,
daylight breaks to vibration of phone,
torso splayed, organs twisted and squeezed.

Harassed limbs scream, struggle into sleeves,
confused agonist muscle, antagonist bone,
curb the sorrow for my loathsome disease.

To support us all, my partner leaves,
her working world a distant zone.
Torso splayed, organs twisted and squeezed.

Dogs eager for walk, grab coat and keys,
socks needle feet, even leather boots groan.
Curb the anger for this invisible disease.

Dishes stacked high, clothes piled to my knees,
curse these aches, dark tunnels through stone.
Heart splayed, lungs twisted and squeezed.

I was a gardener, climbed mountains and trees,
my body now wilts, soil condition unknown.
Curb the sorrow for my loathsome disease,
torso splayed, organs twisted and squeezed.

Blue Marble

We are
dragging our legs
over our neuro degenerative
world. Prescribe: anti-tumour antibiotic.
Amitriptyline, Anthropocene. My asthmatic
lungs wheeze, veins running dry, endless fatigue,
a digestive system bloated and clogged, old growth,
felled and logged. Amitriptyline, Anthropocene. All our
infections afflict this Earth our disturbed dystopian dreams
cause planetary lumbago. Prescribe: Tramadol, Codeine. Hope
prescribed by Attenborough. COVID spreads around the globe.
Creatures extinct and unseen. Amitriptyline. Anthropocene. I
seek an Octopus teacher. Trees down, vertiginous land Stemetil
cease this cyclonic motion. Maxolon ease the heaving oceans.
Cancerous disease consumes this terrain, chemo, radio, super
fried cells, blast them out, we are about obliteration. Human
parasitic taxonomy. Prescribe: Tri-cyclic Amitriptyline.
Disease: Anthropocene. Slow motion human locust
plague. Ballistic missile, nuclear bomb, barren
landscape, chronic pain hits ten. Prescribe:
intravenous morphine. Anthropocene.
Feed the billions factory farmed
Amitriptyline, pesticides
silent spring.

Prayer For A Grey Round Pebble

Bring me back earth, help me replant my garden.
Nurture soil and twig.
Give me hope, brighter than my tiny ember,
chant me the story you know, so I know.

Nurture soil and twig.
Without ever meeting, we are connected.
Chant me the story you know, so I know,
teach me to speak, I will reveal everything.

Without ever meeting, we are connected.
Hold your hand out to me.
Teach me to speak, I will reveal everything.
A grey round pebble lies in your palm.

Hold your hand out to me,
give me hope, brighter than my tiny ember,
a grey round pebble lies in your palm,
help me replant my garden, we are the earth.

Conjecture Written About My Body

Perfect form presents π carried by and imprinted in skin
preconceived   reception
disbelief, total conundrum, perfect body, calculation.

Fatal flaw   bronchial spasm
hairline crack   dysfunctional gut,
perfect face   anxiety   depression.

Convex polygon cyclic
isosceles triangle, masks mangled mind.
Pythagoras, rolls off the tongue.

Conundrum   imperfection   this person seeks
explanation an unknown calculation,
pain is a three-dimensional matrix.

This mouth, short of expression,
side-effect ramification a/fraction,
echoing ricocheting perfect circle calculus.

Primary hyperparathyroidism + hypercalcemia
= revolving door   CT scans, ultrasound, MRI
consultant consideration   % human retraction

+ bone tissue loss calcified organs fraction of pain 8/10
misunderstood + *fibromyalgia x CFS x IBS x FMS*
pain, collapse, sleep   pain, pinned to floor in pain.

Square root deduction disability based on
no solution –
Algebra stumps me at y,   reduction.

Rheumatologist compassion
comprehension addition (+) Duloxetine
this mask conceals (-) subtraction.

Awaiting re-construction
no walks in the park   legs unsteady   no walks
condition < conundrum <

Believe me – Human Services
a/fraction
of whom I used to be.

Music

Inside my soul is music,
mathematics adds, subtracts like atoms

in quiet cadence
my inner light shines and fades –

no matter how dark the lyrics
or task at hand,

from chain gang, slave gang, sailor,
labourer, washerwoman, we sang –

no matter what angel, scoundrel,
pauper, rich man, is outside

the harmony inside makes us one humanity,
clinking to beat and breath of the natural world –

music streaming from the creation of things,
one tribal chant, atom on atom, hammer on anvil,

arrow to the bow,
shooting words from my soul.

The Poet Breaks

If life is a poem when will my stanza end?
I have to break the line, so what follows is new.

If I am whole, cut from concrete,
lapis lazuli sky embraces sunny yellow,
paints the grass green, an easel of words flow
on a turpentine breeze.
When I crack,
adrift in the beauty of abstract, words once loved are suddenly despised.
I am jammed against an embankment marking time, for resolution, the volte
waiting – to imitate,

as the poet breaks.

Hold Me Together I Am Dying To Live

Stitch me in time to cutting incisions,
cross the room with your suture line,
sew me deftly, cocooned in blanket

stitch me. With your elaborate threads of colour
embroider, push me gently through time,
go blind or back, zig zag while running.

Thread a buttonhole around the knot of me,
press needle through linen, through body tissue,
with fingers gloved or cupped in silver.

Feel the pressure of fine steel piercing muscle memory,
repair the seams, ripped flesh unspeakable and torn,
of snapped and cracked bones plain-purl, knit me

use kintsugi. Weave me back and forth, untangle me,
collect earthy reeds and sedges entwine and plait me,
bring serrated margins closer, let them be touching.

Stitch me in time, save nine, my star is dying.
If you have no dexterity *velcro* me, coarsely mend me,
press nylon into waiting room wounds, clasp me.

Hold me together, let our borders touch
our tears soothe the dry need for love,
darn this gash of death, sponge the blood.

Spin the wheel, turn flax to thread, repair me,
stitch the ripped seams of life, lover cradle me,
let our edges be touching.

Pages II

Stuck in my room –
formerly a field,
gnarly old forest,
once wild place.

Longing to wander –
trapped by illness,
barred with rods of iron,
lost to a life with no cure.

Yearn for the breeze –
ache to smell earth,
my hand touches ink,
not the finery of soil.

What has happened here?
My creations upon pages,
my tree companions and me,
pressed into paper.

On The Edge Of A Continent

In a world of moonless nights,
brittle bones splinter, muscles bite.
My lover kept the lanterns burning,
navigated our boat, fastened us with sturdy
rope. Southern ocean storm washed
us overboard, dumped in icy depths,
we wrestled waves, scaled our lurching
vessel, I lay for days on deck –
wake, tend to holes in hull,
bail brine, slow the sinking.
We made it back to shore
to nurse my partner's dying father.
We made it back together.

As You Lay Dying

My heart enlarges to harbour the dead,
blood flowed slow, thickened.
Time and time again, I stood in a funeral line
wishing the silence, the still aching cold
could ferry me to the underworld.

My small child's hand, clasped by priests
and soft eyed aunties grew into an adult hand
curled around a ball of string.
Ropes and riggings of grief lengthening
and unravelling, knotted in disbelief.

We prepare for my father-in-law's looming death.
I surrender to the mundane,
we nurse him, comfort his body.
Accompany his mind to the waterfront,
we hear that final exhalation
as his spirit slips away.

My old ghosts follow his ashes into the sea.
With the tide I grieve.

Exquisite Garden, Lush And Divine

You taught me to love you again –
constant displays, molten orange
and yellow nasturtiums blooming
when I became ill and turned away.

Soil tirelessly tended, now wild
with daisy, fallen seed of parsley,
poppies surround our garden bench –
I linger, craving sun's healing gaze.

Emerging from hibernation, like pollinating
insects my eyes drawn reluctantly
into the throat of your floral universe.
Your tendrils creep in my direction.

Wrestling Chronic Fatigue

Garden of tranquil meditation distorts,
excess coffee to fight sleep of fairy tales,

persistent stupor derails me, an axe of anger
strikes my twitching limbs, half flesh, half wood.

Inside my head resides a tablet carved for survival,
assures me *this moment will pass.* I crave serenity,

babbling brain, vibrating world, I yearn for earth's
silence, to fill myself with water and breathe.

I cry for all that has died, hours escalate and fade,
cling to chance; no fatigue, no pain,

no tattooed permanence, *this moment will pass,*
transform soundlessly at night within dreams.

Plant feet into earth with tree roots, shoot arms
skywards, sprout leaves and move among tree tops.

Reflections, At The Lake

ABC March 15 2019, Christchurch shootings leave 50 people dead after attacks on mosques...

I have come home from hospital, tumour and a parathyroid removed. Seated at Playford Lake, in a haze of anaesthetic. A manmade lake, water source rain, channelled from hillsides. Waterline is low, wish it would rain. Would all the tears I cried be in this lake, fill this lake, long and wide?

I am troubled by senselessness, judgement and murder. I bow my head, imagine each ripple a soul in prayer, a person in their place of peace, or their place of searching. A place where you come to be aware of yourself, connected to earth and sky. A place we all know. Ripples passing over water, immense depth.

This place – ducks and honking fowls splash land, make me laugh, remind me to wonder. Breeze catches the wound on my throat. Bicycle skids in gravel. Galahs fly high, siren squawks pitched to the sky. Coots run across the surface, create little waves, expanding further and further. Shed feathers float like decorations upon a liquid cake. Small dogs bark, *mine* they bark *keep away,* their barks reverberate to the island and back again. A meandering old hound comes over and sniffs, I scratch her head, she leans in. We listen.

What determines a first breath, to live and remain ripples, not act in the realms of chaos? Here with a magpie, some sticks and bark, I contemplate grief, nature, water, the reverberation.

Sherbrooke Forest, November Before The Pandemic

Victorian old growth

Light breaks open dense canopy,

beams through shat ter ing rain

frag ment ed by wind by re-fraction,

reconnects my past and present.

Arboreal family stands to welcome me home,

regaled in bark gowns

of past winters.

Jurassic ferns sprout tightly curled fronds

unravelling contact, revealing change after the decline,

a lacework of rebirth

Lockdown Seasons

Leaf on leaf
layers complete,
daydreams,
coloured constraints,
eucalypt
brown and sturdy.
Crab apple, leaves
in yellows, some tiny.
Paintings of the past,
a gardener's
mistrust of order.
Compounded by
autumn's fall
into days of grey
cold and dreary.
Youth cast aside
in crinkled weary sighs.
Leaf on leaf
caught in evening's
streak of light,
faces fade
from memory.
As buds swell
we dream of spring.

Dreams Of Wild Places

I was seduced by lines of orchard trees dripping
sweet bounty in an earthy rainbow of cherry, apricot,
apple and pear, smells of compost with morning dew.
My small feet loved grandfather's narrow paths
between cabbage and swede, crinkly leaves of green.

Mum's borders of flaring perennials, rhododendrons,
winter fireworks under matted stringy bark.
Layers of tangled undergrowth lured me along tracks
below tree ferns, dark animal fur trunks, tangy musk.

My yearning for the wild and sense of control clashed,
as I used the spade to turn soil, define territory,
twist landscape into sweeps of *pretty* things.
What was this pact I had sworn to the English garden?

Bush crept into my dreams, humus my kidney and liver,
ancient creek water flowed into my veins,
mountain ash roots gnawed the calcium from my bones,
I tossed and turned, woke restless and aching.

Middle-aged feet press into Blundstone boots
scramble over rocky, leaf and bark litter tracks,
passing grey blades of grass tree, matrix of ant mound.
Shadowed by blue gum I struggle with how the light falls,
illness chews away inside, I redefine the maps I had drawn.

Arboreal Dream, Microflora, You And Me

How autumn trees put on a show,
Mardi Gras colour and floats,
after party brown, swept into gutters,
linger in groups at intersections,
we become fragile, withered.

Autumn trees remind me to brace
against cold, as wind and rain blast their core.
When season's last clinging leaf falls,
can they recall the pursuit of light,
sun glimmering, bright green coverings?

Trunk scars and missing limbs,
bleached lightning-struck peaks –
driftwood flagpoles above the canopy.
Below rich leaf mould, roots entwine
stump descendants, fellow trees, microflora,
exchange nutrients, moisture, history.

Moss and lichen costumed tree trunk, spored
to absorb moonlight, taste dawn's dew drops,
embrace photosynthesis, shimmy into spring.
Imprints of botanical memory, a carbon eulogy,
the party never ends.

We all leave a seed, a forest offering.

Postmarked Roseville, *California, USA 9/21/2020*

It arrives in a parcel of brown, her unique handwriting
clear, as in earlier years when she lived in Visalia.
I receive the package with a child's excitement,
note a slight waver in the neat letters.

The shawl inside flows out fills my hands
with instant warmth, radiant blue in sunlight.
Open stitches of textured cobalt, soft as velvet.
Memories rush forward, childhood lessons,
great aunts patiently knitting together our lives.

Uncertain hours sewn together stitch after stitch,
each connecting strand alive with Auntie Barb's story.
Through days of wildfire, riots and pandemic,
separated from her children and friends,
an unknown world for grandchildren emerges.

'Land's End' yarn blended with 'Light Lake Blue'
skeins of colour to embrace and lift our spirits.
Each rope-like thread weaving history and love,
traversed river, deep ocean, brings part of her home.

Night Walk

Confinement and COVID make us edgy,
weighed down with rules of restriction.
I cut a pomegranate, crimson blood spills
from the wound. Ruby gems glimmer
between pale green lettuce leaves.
Warm inside, we devour pasta, salad infused
with herbs and garlic, swallow peppery wine.
Outside clear, crisp with chill, waxing gibbous moon,

cool droplets of night crash against my cheek,
pomegranate explodes in my imagination –
fruit   virus   universe.
Dogs lead the way taking a zig-zag path,
chattering and screeching like galahs
we disturb tawny frogmouth, southern boobook.
Startled eyes flash, reflect the scale of pearly stars
sewn into a dark blue cloth of sky,

a drape touching the sleepers and the waking.
We fall quiet, our four shadows engaged
in the creak of tree limb, rustle of marsupial
within eucalypt canopy. Bats pass overhead
emitting their high frequency signal with wing
flap. Your hand fills mine and squeezes,
our boots roll over the pebble strewn earth,
gentle darkness weaves us into the fabric of life.

In Conversation With Bashō

(Matsuo Kinsaku Bashō 1644-94)

In youth I set off into the high country, to release my mind into wilderness, places we seldom see. Sunshine, snow and rain. Here above the world I try to process the meaning of it all: love and death, the prospect of war, nuclear destruction. Chernobyl still broods today. Meditating on tree and river, wild duck, ant, and ant-eater, grounds me to the place where I exist. Your wisdom, words of beauty, have survived centuries, within the haiku. My Gore-Tex jacket, scratches as I move, assaults my ears, sounds of rain hitting a tin roof as it falls on the hood, unlike the gentle swishing of your grass cape. Leather hiking boots laced up around my ankles leave rugged tread in snow, ooze deep into muddy tracks, squelch me to the present. I am burdened with what has passed since your sandaled feet trod on soft soil, rock and fallen leaf. I suffer long periods of darkness for the blights of our modern world: environmental collapse, over-population, oceans warm and rise, the cycle of nature disrupted. My home close to tamed wilderness is alive with birdcall, enchanting mosses and minute orchids. Kneeling to touch the ochre earth decorated with iron stone and quartz, I hear you. *Learn about a pine tree from a pine tree, and about a bamboo stalk from a bamboo stalk.*

after leaf fall
our weathered nakedness
sprouts a bright flower

Interior Design

My body is a room, pain is furniture. No one comes to stay. Decaying shutters, moth-eaten drapes, rotting French tapestry. Church pew, rough-sawn splintered wood. White ants.

Morbid bookcase, sour walnut wardrobe, discordant grand piano. Rat-gnawed ottomans crown Baltic-pine tall boys, heavy drawers hang over dead house plants, mould obstructed window.

Hypoparathyroidism, calcification, rising damp. Pet-soiled rug. Tattered cushion-less sofa, peeling decoupage side tables, dusty brown posey, cracked glass top, blunt scissors, razor scraper.

Wire framed mattress sags over hand-made desk. Flickering lightbulb. Silverfish infested dictionary. Kidney stones roll around concrete floor. Convex mirrors reflect silent self-blame.

Sounds within four walls, fingernails scratch down black-board. Nerves crawl across chest, down arms. Tarnished doorbell with constant electric hum, sporadic ring – doctor prescribes specialist.

Construct spacious extension, large cedar North facing windows. Reduce calcification from structural areas, residing in organs. Remove tumour, self-blame.

New brass door knocker. Polished timber floor, blue Persian rug.
Rhapis palm, flowering Peace Lily, snoozy sofa, arm chairs,
hand crafted desk. Vase of fresh Alstroemeria.

Open cedar shutters, soft light flows in.

NOTES

Wing Commander Ivan McLeod Cameron, RAF bomber pilot, is believed to be the first Australian to be killed in action during World War II. He was shot down on a reconnaissance flight over Germany on 28 September 1939 and given a German burial. He was my paternal great uncle. Dragstar, was a style of bike, made by Malvern Star, that was popular in the 70s. Salingers's Silver books, Penguin Classics J.D. Salinger, *Franny and Zooey, Raise High the Roofbeams, Carpenters/Seymour, Catcher in the Rye.* Radcliffe Hall, 1928, *The Well of Loneliness.* Robyn Morgan, 1972, *Monster.* 'Pat' Longmore was the proprietor of Kingston Hotel, Richmond, Victoria 1980-86, all lesbian staff, brought in the Lesbian community, but was an 'open' pub. Glasshouse, lesbian pub, Gipps Street Collingwood, Victoria, circa 1991-2011. Cuttersmith, queer, gay, dyke focus, haircutters, Brunswick Street, Fitzroy, Victoria circa 1993-96. Extracts from nursery rhymes, Jack and Jill, Humpty Dumpty, Ring a Ring o' Roses, Rock-a-bye-baby, Mary had a Little Lamb. Drugs mentioned, a mixture of Brand names and main ingredient i.e. amitriptyline is Endep. *Learn about a pine tree from a pine tree, and about a bamboo stalk from a bamboo stalk.* Quote from Bashō as written down by his disciple Doho. Source: Penguin classic 1985, *On Love and Barley Haiku of Bashō* P14.

ACKNOWLEDGEMENTS

To write *The Natural World Somersaults*, I was very fortunate to receive an Arts SA Project Development Grant (2020/2021) from the Department of Premier and Cabinet.

Poems in this collection have been previously published (sometimes in slightly different form) in: *"being" The University of Canberra Vice Chancellor's International Poetry Prize anthology 2023, Pure Slush, Wishbone Words* (UK) , *Jacaranda Journal, Overland Journal, Blue Bottle Journal, Friendly Street Poets Inc Anthology #45, 47, Australian Poetry Journal, Poetica Christi Anthology, "Transition" 2022, InDaily, InReview, Mindshare.org.au writing, Bramble Journal, Cordite, The Mozzie, Poetry D 'Amour Anthology, 2021, Milang Community News, Ship Street Anthology#1* and *Wattletales.*

The following awards were received for versions of poems in *The Natural World Somersaults*: Longlisted Vice Chancellor's International Poetry Prize 2023, *Hold Me Together I Am Dying To Live.* Shortlisted Judith Wright Poetry Prize 2023, *Soft Fruit.* Shortlisted Mindshare SA, Creative Writing Awards 2022, *When Sky Swallows the City.* Second Prize, Positive Words Poetry Competition 2022, *Night Walk.* Second Prize, FAW Lambing Flat Poetry Prize 2021, *Collective Memory.* Shortlisted Robyn Mathison Poetry Competition TSWW 2021, *Dog's Life.* Highly Commended Laura Literary Awards 2021, *Under Winter's Shadow.* Highly Commended Adelaide Plains Poetry Competition 2020, *Seer.* Finalist Goolwa Poetry Cup 2019, *Dreams of Wilderness* and *As You Lay Dying.*

A version of this manuscript was Highly Commended, FSP Single Poets Competition 2021.

I can't thank Ralph Wessman and Walleah Press enough for accepting my manuscript and being so lovely and helpful through the publishing process. One of the best things about writing is the people you meet along the way.

Special thanks to Felicity Plunkett, Rachael Mead and Jude Aquilina. Each of you, as mentor, has played a vital role with so much kindness in the development of this manuscript.

Thanks *Arts SA* for supporting the germination of the project and Rachael Mead for being involved from the beginning. Rachael, your dedication to writing, brilliance and friendship have been galvanizing. Thanks *Writers SA*, Jill Jones, *No Wave*, Gemma and Alex, *Goodwood Books*, Sarah Tooth, Nigel Ford and *Friendly Street Poets*, Martin Christmas for memorable gig photos, *Spoken Word SA*, Caroline *(Unley Yoga)*, Darrin *(Kensington Yoga)*, Emma, Peter and Suzi, (*Studio Flamenco* - palmas and cajon). Without everyone's care and encouragement, rebuilding my language, sense of self and health would have taken years longer.

Thank you to Andrew Noble for the excellent photographic work in replicating my artwork for the cover photo, and Ron Weatherhead for the author's photo. Thanks to my readers Jytte, Fiona Rawson, my sister Simone, Daniel Lyas, Christina, Caroline Reid and Pam Makin. For the dedicated critique and support of Bronwyn Lovell, Lindy Warrell and *Trams End Poets,* Pam Rachootin, Vlad, Valerie, Julie, Martha, Maria Comino, David, Nigel, and Geoff Aitkin, *Kookas*, Ros and Sue, *Chaos with Critique*, such insight, Inez Marrasso and Maria Koukouvas (Vouis). Bruce Greenhalgh and Caroline Reid for our many correspondences.

So grateful to my rheumatologist, Barbara and psychologist, Nicola, for assisting me to live a better life between the episodes of uncontrollable illness.

Thanks to friends and family for your encouragement. Mum (RIP) and Dad for a childhood of books and nature. Dad I appreciate your acceptance of this collection.

None of this would be possible without Helen. Thank you for your tireless edits, proof reads and feedback, especially your love and support, I am constantly amazed by the depth of your heart.

Tes, Morty (in memory) and Ned, always there for a quiet moment, the ear rub and pat.

www.ingramcontent.com/pod-product-compliance
Lightning Source LLC
Chambersburg PA
CBHW061750070526
44585CB00025B/2852
* 9 7 8 1 7 6 3 6 5 3 0 2 3 *